Empathy

ELIZABETH CONDE, LMSW-SIFI

WORD**POWER**

BOOK SERIES BY FIG FACTOR MEDIA

WordPower Book Series

It is sold with the understanding that the publisher and the individual authors are not engaged in the rendering of psychological, legal, accounting or other professional advice. The content and views in each chapter are the sole expression and opinion of its author and not necessarily the views of Fig Factor Media, LLC.

For more information, contact:

Fig Factor Media, LLC | www.figfactormedia.com

Cover Design & Layout by Juan Pablo Ruiz
Printed in the United States of America

ISBN: 978-1-959989-53-0
Library of Congress Control Number: 2023915609

DEDICATION

This book is dedicated to my beautiful daughter Natalie, the light of my eyes. Thanks to you I am the person who I am today. Thank you for being my first editor.

ACKNOWLEDGMENTS

———

I would like to thank Jackie Camacho-Ruiz for giving me the opportunity to be part of the Word Power Book Series. Thank you for believing in me. I would like to thank the Fig Factor staff for your continued support during this process.

I would like to thank all the women in my life who have supported me at all times. Especially my mami, and my sisters who have always believed in me when I did not believe in myself.

I would like to thank my family and friends for always supporting me, mi tribu, love ya!

I would like to thank my Social Work Angels—Ellen, Maria Lizardo, Dr. Cindy Bautista-Thomas, Erica Sandoval, Madeline Maldonado, and Dr. Edith Chaparro—for guiding me through this field. I'm forever indebted to you for your support.

INTRO

I decided to do a book on empathy because ever since I was a child, I have been empathetic. As a child, I witnessed things that would break my heart and would make me cry. When I was younger, I couldn't pinpoint what was going on or name the feeling. As a young adult I came to understand the feeling and the definition.

Empathy is the most popular and powerful word you will hear when you decide to become a social worker. Empathy is the magic tool that must be in your toolbox at all times, which enables you to work with patients, clients, families, and a variety of communities. Anyone can have empathy, not just social workers or professionals in the mental health field. I guess I have been a social worker since my early life and didn't know it.

Empathy is a word made up of seven letters but has so much weight. Empathy can be intense, or it can be light on the heart.

for what is

to be best in a

point of view

Empathy

understand

feelings, th

of another.

what is

WHAT IS EMPATHY?

Empathy is an emotional cognitive response. If we look at the origin of the word empathy, it comes from the Greek word empatheia.

We arrived at the Greek word empatheia, by fusing Em (or in) and pathos (feeling). For the purposes of this book, we'll describe empathy as an emotional understanding leading to guided action.

Empathy is something you can feel in your heart, in your soul, or in your gut. Empathy is being able to understand how someone is feeling.

According to the Merriam-Webster dictionary, the definition of empathy (noun) is:

1. The action of understanding; being aware of, being sensitive to, and vicariously experiencing the feelings, thoughts, and experience of another.

2. The act of imagining one's ideas, feelings, or attitudes as fully inhabiting something observed.

For the purposes of this book, we'll describe empathy as an emotional understanding leading to guided action.

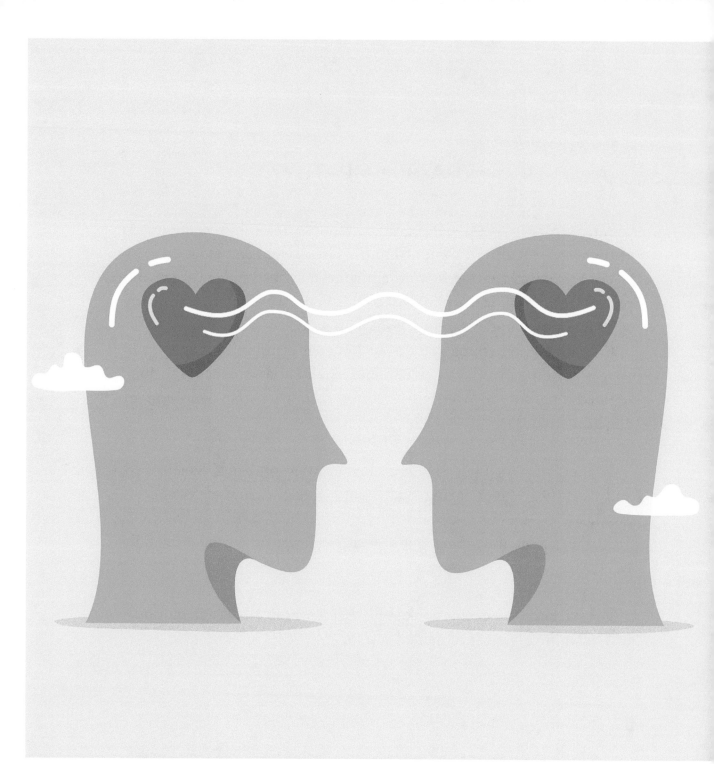

EMPATHY IN TWO PARTS

Empathy is a shared emotion and seeing someone else's perspective.

An example would be your best friend from childhood loses her only child. You love your friend and her child so much you feel that pain as if it was your own. You feel that pain in your heart and gut. This intense empathy we usually feel for our loved ones, our inner circle, or family members.

Seeing things from someone else's point of view is putting yourself in someone else's shoes. An example would be the wildfires that affect California, and you feel so bad for the people there. They have lost everything. You think to yourself that must be devastating, and you feel their pain.

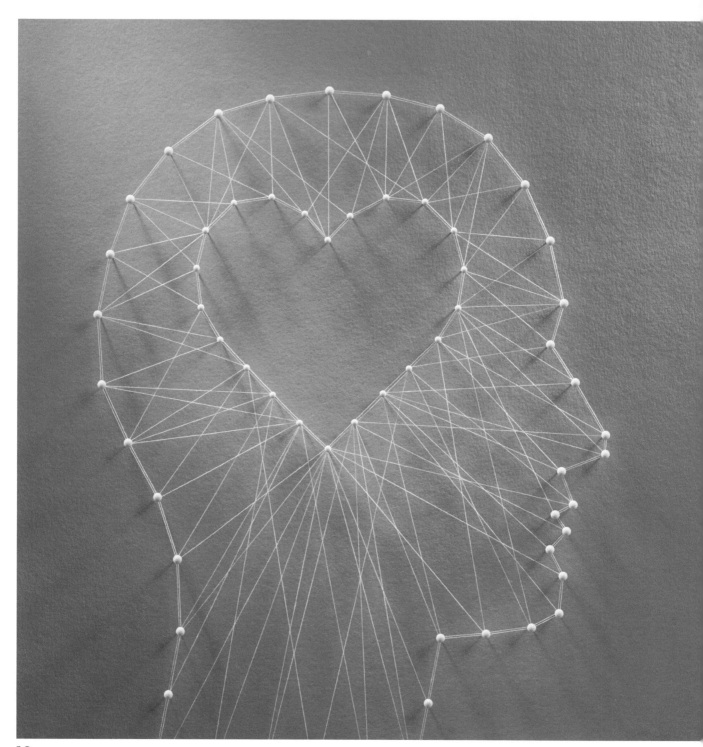

EMPATHY IS NOT...

Empathy is not tangible.

Empathy is not numeric.

Empathy is not visible.

Empathy is not an emotion.

Empathy is not judging.

Empathy is not egocentric.

Empathy is definitely not the same as sympathy.

EMPATHY VS. SYMPATHY

According to the Merriam-Webster dictionary the definition of sympathy (noun) is an affinity, association, or relationship between persons or things wherein whatever affects one similarly affects the other.

For example, if your boss' parent passes away, you feel that it is morally correct to go to the service. You tell your boss you are sorry for their loss.

As we know empathy is….

For example, your best friend just lived through the worst experience of her life and you feel sad. If you had the power to take the pain away, you would.

Empathy is the key ingredient in a healthy relationship. The reason is because there is a connection and there is compassion.

TYPES OF EMPATHY

There are three types of empathy: cognitive empathy, emotional empathy, and compassionate empathy.

Cognitive empathy is putting yourself in someone else's shoes. For example, you work as a part of a team, and you notice two team members are not seeing eye to eye. You try to help them by offering to do mediation between the two of them where they can come to a mutual agreement that would benefit both parties involved.

Emotional empathy is when you feel the other person's emotions. For example, if you see someone cry you may start crying. Your sister just lost her husband, you would empathize with her pain and understand the complex feelings grief can create.

Compassionate empathy is when feeling someone else's pain, but actually moving into an action to help the person. For example, if your best friend does not have money to get to work due to a family emergency, you give your friend money to get work.

EMPATHY FOR YOURSELF & LOVED ONES

Have you ever spoken to yourself in a not polite way? This is not having self-empathy. It happens every day, we forget something or make a mistake and we say, "I'm a _____," and put ourselves down.

How does one empathize with oneself? Be kind to yourself, your brain is listening. All the negative things that we say about ourselves the brain absorbs.

Maybe you have suffered a traumatic event in your life, give yourself grace for surviving the trauma. Be patient with yourself and be kind to yourself. Practice mindfulness, try yoga, exercise, meditation—something that will help you.

Give yourself encouragement. What would you say to a friend that is going through a difficult situation? Direct that answer you would give to your friend towards yourself, have self-compassion.

EMPATHY IN THE WORKPLACE

Leaders need to be empathetic. Why? Because they should lead by example. Leaders work with human beings who have feelings and lives just like they do. The more empathetic the leader is, the better results you get from your employees. The employee morale will be higher as a result of having an empathetic leader.

If an employee feels validated, he won't want to leave the organization and the employees will have greater performance. An example would be giving people at work your undivided attention, respect, and constructive feedback. As a leader, watch out for signs of burnout.

HOW TO BE AN EMPATHETIC PERSON?

Listen without judging.

Listen to understand.

Listen without biases.

Be fully present in the conversation.

Stand up for others.

Model empathy for your loved ones.

Read more about the topic.

EMPATHY IS SOCIAL EMOTIONAL INTELLIGENCE

Social Emotional Intelligence (SEL) is being taught across the United States in schools as I write this book. SEL requires empathy. Research shows that it improves academics, reduces negative social behaviors (i.e., bullying), creates a positive classroom atmosphere and helps students manage everyday life.

Social Emotional Learning is research-based learning which includes the following standards:

1. *Self-awareness*
2. *Self-management*
3. *Social awareness*
4. *Relationship skills*
5. *Responsible decision-making.*

EMPATHETIC LANGUAGE

Empathy recognizes the pain in others. Empathetic people recognize people's non-verbal cues, such as body language. They recognize others' emotions.

Some helpful empathetic statements are:
- *This must be hard for you.*
- *I'm proud of you.*
- *You can count on me.*
- *This must be difficult.*
- *I'm sorry you had to experience that; it must have been frustrating.*
- *Thank you for trusting me with this.*

Some not helpful statements are:
- *Everything happens for a reason.*
- *This too shall pass.*
- *I know how you feel.*
- *He's in a better place now.*
- *Look at the bright side.*

QUOTES FROM LATIN/X SOCIAL WORKERS ON EMPATHY

In my 25 years in the social services field and as a social worker, I've been blessed to meet some amazing leaders and peers. I reached out to a few of these colleagues to share their thoughts on what empathy is.

"Empathy means extending compassion to yourself and others."
- Buddy Whitfield, LCSW, Founder of Beauteous Mind PLLC

"The ability to relate to someone else's pain, hurt, or experience from their vantage point not ours."
- Dr. Carolyn Peguero-Spencer

"Empathy means to be able to understand someone else's feelings and to feel someone else's pain. Regardless of whether you have shared similar life experiences."
- Madeline Maldonado, LCSW-R, Co-Founder of Minette Psychotherapy

"Empathy means showing up for others with an open heart, mind and with open arms."
- Monika Guzman, LMSW

"Empathy means not always understanding another person's internal experience, and still being willing to be curious and ask more, or just bear witness to their experience and know that just being there for them is more than enough."
- Karen Conlon, LCSW, CCATP, Founder of Cohesive Therapy NYC

FINAL THOUGHTS

Practicing empathy is important because it helps build healthy relationships. It is important to succeed in life. It is important for our society as a whole to be empathic towards each other to build a better and peaceful world.

My wish is for a world with more empathy towards each other and more understanding where we can live in harmony.

Imagine we lived in a world without empathy, what would that look like?

ABOUT THE AUTHOR

Elizabeth Conde, LMSW-SIFI, is a bilingual School Social Worker living in New Jersey. She is responsible for providing social, emotional, and academic support for students in her caseload.

For the past 25 years she has worked with different populations and programs, including domestic violence, education, and substance abuse. She is a Modern Abolitionist Professional Volunteer at the Ricky Martin Foundation. She is the Treasurer for the Northern Manhattan Improvement Corporation Advisory Board.

Elizabeth is also a Civics Teacher helping individuals to become U.S. Citizens and be able to exercise their right to vote.

She holds an Associate's Degree in Liberal Arts Psychology from Hudson County Community College, a Bachelor of Arts in Social Work from Rutgers University-Newark, a Master of Social Work from Adelphi University, and her SIFI certification (Seminar Training in Field Instruction) from Columbia University.

Elizabeth's greatest pride is her daughter. Her greatest accomplishment is her daughter graduating with her BFA in Acting.

CONTACT:
condesw@gmail.com
IG: elizabeth_conde_sw

HOW DOES THE WORD **EMPATHY** EMPOWER YOU?